Pick n Mix

Lauren Sophia

BookLeaf Publishing

India | USA | UK

Presentation by *BookLeaf Publishing*

Web: www.bookleafpub.com

E-mail: info@bookleafpub.com

ISBN: 9789358318746

First edition 2024

*To human life and how exquisitely complex
it is.*

PREFACE

Take your pick and get lost in the mix of my small collection of poems on random topics. I wrote this with the purpose of appealing to the big thinkers out there, and to explore the depths of my headspace. It also highlights parts of the 'every day' that we sometimes fail to appreciate fully.

Sonder

the realisation that every single human
has as complex a life as one's own.
A concept that has many mind-blown.

For in our own bubbles we float
and out of that comfort zone
we rarely pop out
because to see through is enough.

So consumed in our own trials
we forget to consider others' tribulations.

And in those thousands
of rushed faces
with lack of
eye contact
lays a million stories
waiting to be uncovered.

It's important to take a minute
to sit back and people-watch
watching the way the world works
and that every individual

is a piece of the jigsaw.

Smudged

If you asked me to describe myself
I would struggle to think of much.

I'm pretty sure I'm tall and slender,
my surface made of glossy glass,
sometimes smudged,
sometimes smashed.

My simplicity magnifies
everyone else around me
for I have minimal features
yet my purpose is to accentuate
the features of others.

See, when people look at me
they simply see a duplicate,
for I have no originality
I simply become my surroundings.

I am mute
as i helplessly watch people
stare at me in frustration
and i try to scream and shout that they are
exquisite the way they are

but I stay silently stiff and cold in my wooden
frame.
Daily I get to witness complex works of art
sell themselves short.

Will i ever know what I look like
to be able to understand my best angles
like the mannequins that pose
in front of me?

Will i ever view my own reflection?
Maybe i too would turn away in rejection.

Nostalgia FM

You are now listening to Nostalgia FM
so tune in with me.

To a time where we were free.
Let's leave adulting behind
and travel back to peace of mind.
I'm happy we experienced an
organic childhood,
full of fresh air and
not the freshest tech.

Playing out with your friend
from down the road
whether it was sunny or cold,
rushing in to the house to down some
juice then you're back out, all that running
around had you doing daily workouts.

So excited for the family road trips
your parents' favourite albums playing
in the car, no skips.
Learning every song word for word
until you know it better then them
and then they ask 'what do you know about
this?'

The sun's rising outside
Milkshake is on TV, it's 6am and you
spring out of bed cos tiredness doesn't
exist and a minute can't be missed.
Wake up shake up time at primary school,
dancing in sync with your class not caring about
looking a fool.
The real test of trust was playing heads down
thumbs up,
and you'd try to sneak peek who's shoes were
who's close up.

You search for the cleanest whiteboard in the
pack, sniffing the pens and glue behind
everyone's back.
Your biggest flex was getting your pen licence
or winning a game of sleeping lions.
Running under that multicoloured parachute
hoping to make it to the other side.

You couldn't wait to get home and watch your
favourite shows on CBBC back to back,
Horrible Histories, Charlie + Lola, Art Attack.
Bedtime Stories on CBeebies as a lullaby,
you look up to the ceiling with a happy sigh
thinking you just couldn't beat this day,
but you'd try.

That den you built in your room
full of blankets and imagination
could never be broken,
so you could hide in there forever
and never be awoken.
Studying music videos like they were movies,
rehearsing every step and
storing it for performance time.

Trying to be as quiet as possible when
the TV's on cos it was a school night,
being successful at staying up till 10:30 thinking
you was the coolest kid on sight.

The big link up with the cousins
at your grandparents,
and yeah you had a favourite
and with them you made memories,
you just wish you could save it.
The weekly fix of pick n' mix,
eating them till you felt sick.

Your CD rom collection went crazy
that folder was stacked
had it for years and it was still in tact.
Planning all your purchases as you flick through
the Argos catalogue
from the Nintendo DS to the Wii,
you wanted both cos for you

there was no fees
and your parents would repeat that
money doesn't grow on trees.

All of a sudden, you're not flicking
through the catalogue anymore
but it's an old photo album.
As you look and laugh at a time
when your only objective was to have fun.
Yet you yearned to be older
wishing to be 10, 15, 20
you didn't know the stresses that come
with age, and trust me there's plenty.

It's funny how things change
cos i really wanted to grow up
but now i just want to be a kid again.

Why can't the sweet smell of nostalgia
be our forever,
enjoying every day whatever the weather.
And as you close the photo album
you think to yourself, life goes on,

but at least we have these memories
to treasure.

Enigma

My favourite enigma
I'm so intrigued.

You're a book I cannot put down.
I need to find out what happens next
reading eagerly between the lines of text.

Yet, this tale is unclear
the dots I cannot connect
so the storyline I try to dissect,
and that's what keeps me flicking
through each page.

I don't even need a bookmark
I'm too far in to pause at this stage.

So I will continue to enjoy the mystery of you.

Swirl of Identity

Let me trace the maze of your fingerprint and
see where it leads to.

This swirl of identity fascinates me as it spirals
into one.

How can something so faint be so incriminating,
so significant?

It's coding was only written once.
Each has its own little quirk.

I can't help but be left in awe of the Artist
that crafted each intricate line

with such care.

Spectrum

Did you see the sunset today?

I did.

I watched it drown into the landscape and
speckle the sky,
boasting a warm shade of amber that
transformed into a tangerine tantrum.

With millions of mesmerised eyes
gazing at its every move
it started to blush a delicate pink.

Well, another day is complete
and as the skies turn into a navy blue sheet,

sunrise can't wait to have it's time to shine.

Bloodline

Siblings
can be as contrasting as day and night,
sugar and spice.

The introvert vs the extrovert.
The nonchalant vs the one
who's feelings are easily hurt.
Yet they share so much -
clothes (occasionally), parents, secrets.
The floor you both took your first steps on,
the walls that witnessed you sprout
from birth,
growing up on the same turf.

Seeing you in your 'popping to the corner shop
outfit' on a daily,
Hair in the same recycled messy bun.
Oh and your embarrassing moments?
They've seen a ton.
Reminding you of them and replaying them
constantly to make fun.
In fact the both of you have enough
incriminating footage
to blackmail each other,

but you've stashed it away for the compilation
on their wedding day.

You could write a book on the inside jokes
those daily catchups,
those movie nights.
Shouting 'what snacks we got'
as you take an hour to settle
on a film you both won't lose interest in within
10 seconds.

But let's not pretend with siblings it's all
sunshine and rainbows,
both wearing halos,
no cons all pros.
You will step on each others toes.
Things will irritate you, even if they're micro.
Started off arguing about
who gets the remote
and see these petty arguments you may never
outgrow.
But at the end of the day you know
love will always follow.

But siblings are not always
connected by blood.
There can a brother or sister in someone who
you're not related to but, you relate to.
Related in personality, life experiences, faith.

A friend that sticks closer than a brother like the
Proverb says right,
knowing full well they're holding onto that bond
tight.
And their loyalty isn't the
'here today gone tomorrow' type
but they're the type to stick around for life.

See, siblings know more than just your
Instagram highlights,
they know all the hidden
interludes inbetween.
They witness the rollercoaster of
your daily life,
sometimes right on the ride beside you
the high climbs, the sharp bends
and the steep drops.

It's cool to have another version of you walking
around in an alternate shell,
who gets you inside out and knows you
so well.

So this a shout to them,
having siblings is a gem.

Stutterflies

When i think of you

sorry
let me start again

When i think of you
i can't think of a second line
for your presence in my mind alone
has me
at a loss for words.

So seeing you in person?
Pshhh.
I find my instincts battling over the right thing to
say and do.
My usual personality stammers,
you could call it stutterflies.

The way it takes control
is a mixture of frustrating but fun.

There's just something about
the rush of a crush.

Wash Day

Saturday was hair day.

It was my mom's full time job
to maintain my mane with my head
rested on her lap,
as she went through bobbles
that would pop
attempting to keep this thick hair at bay.

Then secondary school started,
and the time came for me to
begin doing it myself.
Mate, will all the products I needed
it would've helped if I'd have been abundant in
wealth.

Binge watching YouTube videos,
the 2a's to the 4c's,
like learning your ABCs,
curl patterns can come in 3s.

Washing my hair was basically a 9-5,
clocking it was moisture that made it thrive.
Detangling from the bottom to top,
or else it would all be a flop.

That part would make my arms burn
then came stylings' turn.

Tryna get my fro to look a cute wash n' go,
flooding my curls with Aunt Jackie's cream,
all for it to look more like a frizz n' go.

Wanting my curls to look like the other girls
cos it took a while to embrace mine,
to love my awkward spirals
to accept that they were just fine.

My fro speaks volumes,
sometimes a lot less then me.
It almost feels people see my hair
before they see me,
but i quite like that

cos it will always be a part of my identity.

It's a Breeze

As i enjoy the gentle breeze
I think about how it can

switch

from calming to catastrophic in seconds,
taking down anything and everything that dares
to come in its path with no mercy.

It delicately dances with the trees
but can also rip them out from the roots
like a plug pulled from a socket.

The wind is invisible
yet its power is
undeniable

and it makes sure to be seen.

Harmony

No need to translate,
this language transcends all borders.

A common love shared worldwide.
One simple lyric recognised instantly
or a beat drop that strikes a chord
with any crowd.

For a moment
the world is in sync
singing the same melody.

There's Plenty More Fish

There's a whole other world in the sea

But we've only paddled in the possibilities,
only dipped a toe in the depths.

We had Finding Nemo
but what else are we yet to find
in the deep blue?

Sparkling delicately in the sun rays,
the stillness so serene
it's easy to forget the sheer supremacy it holds
how it can consume so effortlessly and
oh-

By marvelling at the magnitude of the ocean my
mind has
drifted off
with the

current

and I'm miles out.

Time to anchor myself and come back to shore.

Isn't it Ironic

It's quite ironic
that I'm attempting to write a poem
about feelings I can't put into words.

Ask me what's wrong
and I'll struggle to articulate.
You may lose patience having to wait
as I contemplate
how to put it so you'd understand.

This brain fog needs to clear
so i can see through this misty wilderness.
My motivation is running out of ink
as I force myself to scribble.

Yet as my pen touches the paper,
I feel my passion bubbling back.
My ideas take over
and the pen can't keep up with my brain.

It unlocks the gate
that suppresses inner battles
I'd rather not talk about out loud.

But it airs it all out on paper.

I still couldn't really tell you
how I felt when i started this poem
but I know I feel better now.

At least I know how I feel about that.

Mini-me

My my,
how time does fly
cos now 18 years have gone by.

As i flick through
the vivid timeline of your life,
I go back to the beginning
when you first arrived and I smiled
cos you had the same eyes as me.

But then my eyes were opened
to the reality that being a mom
offers no annual leave.
My eyes are half shut at 3am
trying to console you,
and then I start to cry
because you won't stop crying,
but I'd still take it over any 9-5.

All of a sudden you are two,
doing more than coo and chew
you're talking and walking,
- but not too far now.

Why can't you be 4,

face lighting up when you hear the
ice cream van.

I miss when you were 8,
and your joy was to be my mini-me,
my shadow.

Then the pre-teens dawned
on the both of us.
I delve into when you were twelve,
sneaking into my room
to experiment with makeup,
and I wish I could conceal you
from the self-conscious era
you're about to enter.

Then you were 14,
and I could never have foreseen
how different things would be.

Long are the days
you would follow me around;
now you isolate yourself in your four walls.
You think I'm always complaining
but I'm just training
you for your life ahead.

To be honest, I get it
as when I was 14

I was exactly the same way,
not really grasping
what my parents had to say.

Oh, then you've turned 16
and you're leaving school,
but not me - not yet.

So here we have it, the present day.
You're 18,
going on your first girls' holiday
and I struggle to keep my
panicked sick feelings at bay
because with me I want you to stay

but I also want you to have new experiences
and witness the wonderful sights worldwide.

I've had the privilege of watching
you grow up,
so beautiful and smart
now it's time for your adulthood to start.

But just know
no matter how far you roam,
here you'll always have

a mom and a home.

Auburn

There's something
so calming about Autumn

some would say it has bought them
peace.

The gentle crunch as you step
through the auburn yellow blanket,
that dazzles the ground in
a variety of pigmentations,
you have no choice but
to admire this creation.

Trees preparing for 'new year new me'
as they shed their yearlong leaves
and because of the loss, it grieves
but fresh foliage it will receive.

A 'warm up' to the wintery cold,
we watch as the next season unfolds.

SPF

The sporadic splashes
satisfy your ears,
excited kids jump into the pool
baking in the sun, in need of refreshment.

Another sound to compliment is laughing and
chattering bouncing through the air,
everyone schedule-free
and without a care.

Sun beds scrape the floor
as those dedicated to tanning
migrate to the rays.

Sitting on the balcony,
snacking on crisps and sipping,
taking in the view.
This is what you've seen in the pictures;
but this time it's right in front of you.

Evening strolls with that distinct warming
scent has you so laidback
as you search for the best gifts
and souvenirs to take back.

Palm trees as plentiful as people
whilst the clouds hide behind
the bright baby blue.
Clear sky, clear mind,
open to new ways of life and culture.

You eagerly go to sleep
knowing another day awaits

as great as this one.

Constellations

I'm playing connect the dots
with the vast twinkles in the sky
but i don't think I'll ever finish this game.

For just when you believe it's nearly complete,
a new array starts to shine through.

They say the more you look
the more you can see.
It's mind boggling to comprehend
how many of the rarest of diamonds
occupy the atmosphere.

This is why i feel
that stars are like people.
Billions of them exist
and from far away they can look the same
but they each hold their own -

own name
own individuality,
own galaxy.

With only a momentary glance
you can create a whole assumption

of a person.
But it's when you gaze past the surface,
get out your telescope,
you magnify an individual's story.

What constellation are you from?
I ask both the stars and humans alike.

Kill Them With Kindness

Kill them with kindness
is something i cannot do
cos I'm too nice for that.

'Oh she won't mind'
the one that lets it slide
even when she feels a way inside
call me a playground.

Spin my head around like a carousel
until I'm dizzy, but if you ask
I'll say I'm well.
But don't go too crazy, I've been
blessed with the curse of sensitivity
which gives me the ability
to feel at a higher intensity.

A single scratch leads to an open wound
and as it bleeds i warn myself to not take things
so personally the next time,
but clearly that didn't happen
cos I'm writing this rhyme.

Forget money,
my investments are energy and emotions,

and I've been scammed more than once
and I'd try to change the ending each time,
yet it's the same plot.

Serving a whole banquet
in exchange for a crumb
and still feeling full.
Yes there's more happiness
in giving than receiving,
but this is just thieving
and I'm left stranded, empty handed.
Yet I'll somehow still celebrate it.

Seeing individuals through
rose tinted glasses,
all people get passes
cos i have an affinity with
seeing the good in everybody.
Red flags gracefully float in the wind
alarm bells are just faint whispers
and i fail to spot the bad
as i paint everyone
how i choose to see them
with my pretty selection of colours.

Maybe we all have a quality
that we'd like to change
a part of our personality we'd rearrange.

But I'm coming to realise that each of our
makeups are meant to be that way,
and the way we function is here to stay.

Maybe you're an empath, over-thinking,
people-pleasing sensitive chic like myself,
or maybe you'd leave those qualities
on the shelf.
See, under the same cookie cutter
we're not all gonna fit
but what we have in common is the right
to feel the way we choose to feel
and heal the way we choose to heal.

You might think I'm dramatic
and certain situations I'd go crazy in
you'd be static.
But once you accept we're all different, you've
cracked it.

And instead of letting these
characteristics go sour,
use them as a superpower.
Because these are what make you unique
and without them you are weak

So please, keep letting your originality speak.

There's Something About Sundays

Sunday is a day to unwind
as you put that jazz record on rewind
from the likes of Ella Fitzgerald to Billie
Holiday
all the classics lined up to play,
that snazzy saxophone
effortlessly blowing you away.

Sunday is a day for eating,
eating real good.
Sitting round the table
with a wholesome Sunday roast
coming in a variety of versions.
Whether it's with or without rice,
mac n cheese,
honey parsnips, crispy roast potatoes
and Yorkshire p's,
take your pick.

Sunday is a day for family,
to chill by the fire
playing cards
or watching a guilty pleasure movie
you've seen countless times

as you all recite your favourite lines.

Sunday is a day to reset
sipping on a beverage of your choice
as you clock out from this week
and prepare to check in
to the week ahead.

Sunday is a favourite for many.
Couldn't say the same for Monday.